D1708263

# WHAT IS THE ATMOSPHERE?

JOE GREEK

996

L 1005

1012

Britannica
Educational Publishing
IN ASSOCIATION WITH
ROSEN
EDUCATIONAL SERVICES

Published in 2015 by Britannica Educational Publishing (a trademark of Encyclopædia Britannica, Inc.) in association with The Rosen Publishing Group, Inc.
29 East 21st Street, New York, NY 10010

Distributed exclusively by Rosen Publishing.
To see additional Britannica Educational Publishing titles, go to rosenpublishing.com.

First Edition

**Britannica Educational Publishing**
J.E. Luebering: Director, Core Reference Group
Mary Rose McCudden: Editor, Britannica Student Encyclopedia

**Rosen Publishing**
Hope Kilcoyne: Executive Editor
Jeanne Nagle: Editor
Nelson Sá: Art Director
Nicole Russo: Designer
Cindy Reiman: Photography Manager

**Library of Congress Cataloging-in-Publication Data**

Greek, Joe.
What is the atmosphere?/Joe Greek. — First edition.
     pages cm — (Let's find out! Weather)
Includes bibliographical references and index.
ISBN 978-1-62275-783-1 (library bound) — ISBN 978-1-62275-784-8 (pbk.) —
ISBN 978-1-62275-785-5 (6-pack)
1. Atmosphere — Juvenile literature. 2. Weather — Juvenile literature. I. Title.
QC863.5.G73 2015
551.5 — dc23
                                                                                              2014024365


*Manufactured in the United States of America*

**Photo credits:** Cover, interior pages Robert Adrian Hillman/Shutterstock.com; p. 4 Courtesy, Image Science & Analysis Laboratory, NASA Johnson Space Center, No. ISS001-421-24; p. 5 Jimmy Tran/Shutterstock.com; p. 6 Osvaldru/Shutterstock.com; pp. 7, 9, 15, 16, 18 Encyclopædia Britannica, Inc.; p. 10 David H. Harlow/U.S. Geological Survey; p. 12 Joe Raedle/Getty Images; p. 13 © valdezrl/Fotolia; p. 14 iLexx/E+/Getty Images; p. 17 Nick Impenna/Photo Researchers; p. 19 fishco/Moment/Getty Images; p. 20 © Merriam-Webster Inc.; p. 21 Chris Valle/Moment/Getty Images; p. 22 ChinaFotoPress/Getty Images; p. 23 NASA Goddard Space Flight Center/Scientific Visualization Studio; p. 25 © Barbara Whitney; p. 26 Jet Propulsion Laboratory/NASA; p. 27 NASA/JPL/Space Science Institute; p. 28 MarcelClemens/Shutterstock.com; p. 29 NASA.

# CONTENTS

# Earth's Protective Shell

Many planets, including Earth, have a protective layer of gases called an atmosphere.

Earth's atmosphere helps keep the planet warm enough for living things to survive. It also protects life on the planet from meteoroids and from certain harmful rays from the Sun and other stars.

From outer space, layers of the atmosphere become visible.

The atmosphere makes life on Earth possible. Not only does it keep us warm, but it holds the oxygen that animals use to breathe. Other gases in the atmosphere help plants survive as well.

A **meteoroid** is a chunk of rock or metal from space. Most meteoroids burn up as they pass through the atmosphere before they can hit the planet.

Without the atmosphere, farms would not be able to make food.

# LAYERS OF THE ATMOSPHERE

Scientists divide the atmosphere into five layers. The layer closest to Earth is the troposphere. It extends up to 11 miles (18 kilometers) at its highest point above Earth's surface.

The second layer is the stratosphere, which extends to about 30 miles (50 kilometers) above the surface. The stratosphere contains the ozone layer. The ozone layer blocks some of the harmful rays that come from the Sun. These rays can cause skin cancer, eye diseases, and other health problems in people and other animals.

The third layer is the mesosphere. It extends up

The clouds you can see in the sky are located in the troposphere.

to about 50 miles (80 kilometers) above Earth's surface. The fourth layer, the thermosphere, ranges from about 50 to 300 miles (80 to 480 kilometers) above Earth.

The fifth and highest layer is the exosphere. This layer ends where Earth's gravity is too weak to prevent particles of gas from drifting into space.

**Gravity** is a pulling force that makes all objects attract other objects. On Earth gravity pulls objects toward the center of Earth. This is what makes objects fall. It is also what gives objects weight.

This drawing shows what can be found in each layer of the atmosphere.

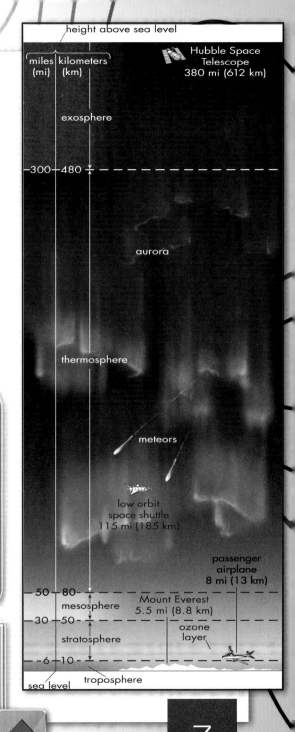

height above sea level

miles kilometers
(mi) (km)

Hubble Space Telescope
380 mi (612 km)

exosphere

-300-480

aurora

thermosphere

meteors

low orbit space shuttle
115 mi (185 km)

passenger airplane
8 mi (13 km)

50 - 80-
mesosphere

Mount Everest
5.5 mi (8.8 km)

30 - 50-

ozone layer

stratosphere

-6 -10-

sea level

troposphere

# A Mix of Gases

Earth's atmosphere consists of several gases, as well as small liquid and solid particles. The gases include nitrogen, oxygen, argon, carbon dioxide, helium, and water vapor. The atmosphere is about three-fourths nitrogen and one-fifth oxygen.

Gravity pulls the heavier elements, such as nitrogen and oxygen, closer to Earth's surface. Lighter elements,

People need oxygen. Since they cannot breathe in oxygen from the air, deep-sea divers use tanks that hold oxygen.

including helium and hydrogen, are more common higher in the atmosphere.

In the lower regions of the atmosphere, weather patterns and wind evenly mix the gases. In the higher regions, elements are less mixed.

This chart shows that elements weigh more when they are closer to the ground.

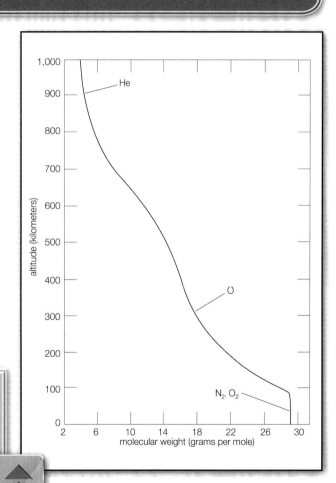

# How the Atmosphere Formed

Scientists are not certain how Earth's atmosphere formed. However, they believe it was the result of gases released from inside the planet and from tiny organisms, or living things.

More than 4 billion years ago, people would have been unable to live on Earth. The early atmosphere lacked

Gases from volcano eruptions may have helped form the atmosphere.

the amount of oxygen that people need to survive. At that time, the only organisms on Earth were anaerobic. This means they could survive without oxygen.

In time, some organisms developed photosynthesis. Photosynthesis is a process that allows organisms, such as plants, to produce their own food. Through photosynthesis, organisms take in energy from sunlight. They use this light energy to change water and a gas called carbon dioxide into oxygen and nutrients called sugars. The oxygen is released into the air. As a result, oxygen built up in the atmosphere over time.

**THINK ABOUT IT**
We breathe in the oxygen that trees and other plants produce. What would happen if forests suddenly disappeared?

Organisms like this tiny synechococcus added oxygen to the atmosphere as it was forming.

# Understanding Weather

Weather is the daily state of the atmosphere. Earth's weather occurs mainly within the troposphere. Weather is important because it affects people's comfort, food supply, and safety.

There are five features in the atmosphere that combine to create weather. The first is temperature, or how hot or cold it is outside. Wind, the movement of air across Earth's surface, is the second feature. The third feature, humidity, is

**Wind can be a gentle breeze or powerful gusts that knock down trees.**

**THINK ABOUT IT**
Meteorologists warn people of dangerous weather. What types of weather can be harmful?

Lightning is electricity released from Earth's atmosphere during thunderstorms.

the amount of moisture in the air. Precipitation, such as rain, snow, and sleet, is the fourth feature. The last feature, atmospheric pressure, is the weight of the air.

Scientists who study weather are called meteorologists. They pay attention to the features in order to predict what the weather will be like in a few hours or a few days. Thunderstorms, for example, can be expected when changes in atmospheric pressure occur.

# ATMOSPHERIC PRESSURE

The weight of the air is known as atmospheric pressure. It is also called barometric pressure. The gases in the air are made of particles called molecules. The molecules are pulled toward Earth by gravity. The pressure is therefore greatest at sea level. There, the gas particles are pressed together by the weight of the air above them.

Barometric pressure is measured with a barometer.

Air becomes lighter farther away from Earth's surface. This is because the air molecules are always moving.

Those farthest away from the surface have more room to move. They can spread out more so there is less pressure on them.

As this graph shows, atmospheric pressure gets weaker as we move away from the ground.

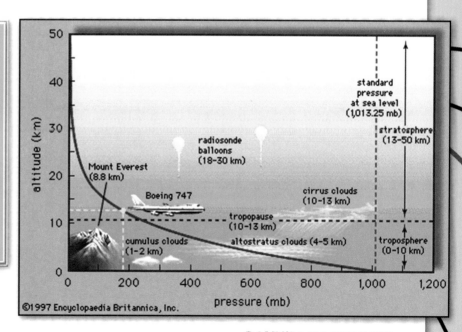

©1997 Encyclopaedia Britannica, Inc.

# THE FORMATION OF CLOUDS

Water in oceans, lakes, rivers, streams, and ponds on Earth evaporates, or turns into a gas, when it is heated. That gas is called water vapor. It rises into the air. The amount of water vapor that air can hold depends on the air's temperature. The cooler the air, the less water it can hold. As air cools, some of the water vapor condenses, or turns back into

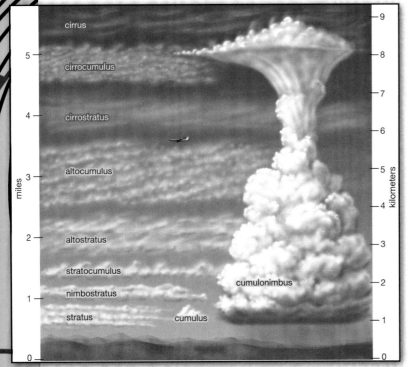

cirrus

cirrocumulus

cirrostratus

altocumulus

altostratus

stratocumulus

nimbostratus

stratus

cumulonimbus

cumulus

miles

kilometers

**Various types of clouds form at different heights.**

a liquid. It forms visible water droplets. When the droplets come together they form clouds. Once formed, clouds remain until the air warms or until the droplets become so large and heavy that they fall to the ground as precipitation.

Meteorologists identify clouds mainly by appearance. The three main types of clouds are cirrus, cumulus, and stratus. Cirrus are high, thin clouds made of ice crystals. Cumulus are puffy clouds that often look like mountains. Stratus clouds are layered.

**THINK ABOUT IT**
How many forms of precipitation can you name?

Cirrus clouds may look almost straight or slightly curved.

17

# WHY THE SKY IS BLUE

The Sun's rays that stream down to Earth appear as white light. White light is made up of all the colors of the spectrum, and each color has a different wavelength. For instance, red has a longer wavelength than blue has. As the Sun's rays pass through the atmosphere, they are reflected and bent by air molecules and dust particles.

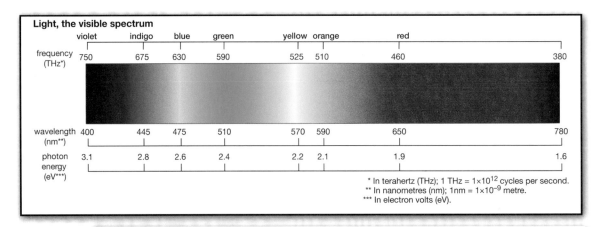

**Light, the visible spectrum**

| | violet | indigo | blue | green | | yellow | orange | | red | |
|---|---|---|---|---|---|---|---|---|---|---|
| frequency (THz*) | 750 | 675 | 630 | 590 | | 525 | 510 | | 460 | 380 |
| wavelength (nm**) | 400 | 445 | 475 | 510 | | 570 | 590 | | 650 | 780 |
| photon energy (eV***) | 3.1 | 2.8 | 2.6 | 2.4 | | 2.2 | 2.1 | | 1.9 | 1.6 |

\* In terahertz (THz); 1 THz = $1 \times 10^{12}$ cycles per second.
\*\* In nanometres (nm); 1nm = $1 \times 10^{-9}$ metre.
\*\*\* In electron volts (eV).

**The colors we are able to see are different because of their wavelengths.**

The short blue light waves get absorbed by particles in the atmosphere. The blue light gets scattered, or bounced from particle to particle, in a process called diffusion. This causes the sky to appear blue.

Light travels in the form of a wave. The **wavelength** is the distance between two peaks of the wave.

If the wavelength of blue was longer, the sky might be another color.

# THE GREENHOUSE EFFECT

The greenhouse effect is a warming of Earth's surface and the air above it. It is caused by gases in the air that trap energy from the Sun. These gases are called greenhouse gases. The most common greenhouse gases are water vapor, carbon dioxide, and methane.

Land, oceans, and plants absorb, or

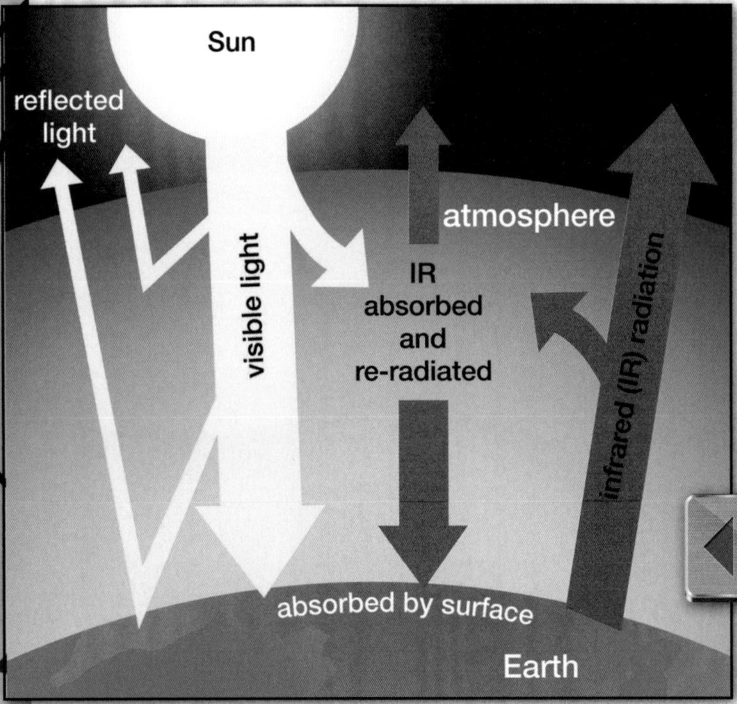

**Energy from sunlight must escape or become stuck in the atmosphere.**

Sun

reflected light

atmosphere

visible light

IR absorbed and re-radiated

infrared (IR) radiation

absorbed by surface

Earth

soak up, energy from sunlight. They release some of this energy as heat. Greenhouse gases absorb the heat and then send it back toward Earth. Without greenhouse gases, this heat would escape back into space.

Scientists believe that human activities are increasing the power of the greenhouse effect. When people drive a car or operate a factory they burn coal, oil, and other fossil fuels. This adds extra greenhouse gases to the air, and the extra gases trap more heat. Scientists think that this has led to global warming, or a steady rise in the average temperature of Earth's surface.

**THINK ABOUT IT**

What would happen to life on Earth if there were no greenhouse gases in the atmosphere?

Oil refineries release large amounts of gases into the atmosphere.

# AIR POLLUTION

Air pollution happens when harmful substances are released into the air. Wildfires, volcanoes, and chemicals from factories cause some air pollution. But most air pollution comes from burning fossil fuels. These include coal, oil, and natural gas. Factories, electrical plants, and automobiles use these fuels for power. When the fossil fuels are burned they release solid particles, such as ash and soot, into the air. Harmful gases may also be released. This type of pollution is often seen as smog over cities. Smog-filled air is hazy, or hard to see through.

In addition, some kinds of air pollution cause global warming. Scientists have discovered that

◀◀ Pollution, such as smog, can lead to health problems for people.

the average surface temperature on Earth is slowly rising. Higher temperatures could cause polar ice caps to melt. This would cause sea levels to rise. Plants, animals, and buildings along coastlines would be in danger. Some forms of air pollution are also harmful to the ozone layer in the stratosphere. The ozone layer is important because it protects Earth against harmful rays from the Sun.

**THINK ABOUT IT**
**What machines and technology do you see daily that burn fossil fuels?**

The purple in this image is a hole in the ozone layer above Antarctica. It was caused by pollution.

# PROTECTING THE ATMOSPHERE

Global warming and air pollution can cause problems for the future. The rising temperatures may lead to changes in rain patterns. This could bring about flooding in some areas and drought in others. Both drought and flooding could hurt farmers. Drought can be a problem in forests because it increases the danger of forest fires. Coastal flooding caused by rising sea levels may force many people to move closer inland.

Many scientists and governments, however, are

Rising temperatures have caused large glaciers, or ice sheets, to melt.

**COMPARE AND CONTRAST**

**What are some problems caused by drought? How are they different than problems caused by too much rain?**

working to reduce the damage people have caused. Some governments have passed laws that require factories and companies to reduce the amount of pollutants they put into the air. Some companies and individuals are working to develop new ways to use other sources of energy, such as solar power and wind-generated electricity. These sources do not pollute as much as burning fossil fuels does.

People can reduce their own use of fossil fuels by taking public transportation, such as buses and trains, or by riding bicycles instead of driving cars.

Geothermal power plants use heat from inside Earth to generate power. They are one of many alternatives to fossil fuels.

# OTHER ATMOSPHERES

Earth's atmosphere is special because it can support plant and animal life. It protects people from the Sun's harmful rays. It contains the right amounts of gases that are needed to breathe. It prevents Earth from becoming too cold or too hot.

There are eight planets and more than 160 moons in our solar system, so there are many different kinds of

The thick clouds of Venus's atmosphere hide the harsh surface below.

Saturn's largest moon, Titan, is the only moon known to have a thick atmosphere. ▶▶

atmospheres. For instance, Venus has a thick atmosphere. Its surface temperatures are about 867°F (464°C), making it too hot for life as we know it to exist. In contrast, the atmosphere on Mars is very thin. Carbon dioxide makes up about 95 percent of the atmosphere of Mars. It would be impossible for animals to breathe on Mars.

The **solar system** consists of the Sun and everything that orbits, or travels around, the Sun. This includes the eight planets and their moons, dwarf planets, and countless asteroids, comets, and other small, icy objects.

# A Unique Planet

Earth is one of countless objects in the universe. Still, scientists have not yet discovered any place like it. Its unique atmosphere is what allows life to thrive. It makes it possible for children to play in the snow and for farmers to grow crops.

Scientists have discovered many planets and moons that have atmospheres. Some have the same gases that

Earth's atmosphere protects the planet's many environments, from snow-covered mountains to deserts.

Earth has, including water vapor. Scientists have even seen lightning on Jupiter and Saturn. No other atmosphere, however, comes close to matching Earth's. Without its unique atmosphere, Earth would be just another object spinning in space.

**THINK ABOUT IT**

What do you think is the most important thing the atmosphere does for Earth?

Our atmosphere makes it possible for us to breathe, play, and enjoy our world.

# GLOSSARY

**air** The invisible mix of gases that surrounds Earth.

**anaerobic** Able to live without oxygen.

**condenses** Changes from a gas into a liquid.

**evaporates** Changes from a liquid into a gas.

**food supply** Available food production for a population.

**greenhouse effect** Warming of Earth's surface and part of the atmosphere caused by gases in the air that trap heat.

**meteorologists** Experts that study and predict weather.

**organism** A living thing, such as an animal, a plant, or a single-celled life-form.

**oxygen** A gas that all animals need to breathe.

**particle** A small piece of something, such as dust.

**photosynthesis** A process that uses sunlight to make food from carbon dioxide and water.

**polar ice caps** Sheets of ice that form around the North and South Poles.

**precipitation** Liquid and solid forms of water, such as rain, snow, and sleet, that fall to the ground from clouds.

**rays** Streams of energy that enter the atmosphere from outer space.

**smog** Fog or haze that is combined with air pollutants.

**water vapor** Water in a gaseous form especially when below boiling temperature and spread through the atmosphere.

# FOR MORE INFORMATION

## Books

Gosman, Gillian. *What Do You Know About Earth's Atmosphere?* New York, NY: PowerKids Press, 2013.

Lawrence, Ellen. *What Is Weather?* New York, NY: Bearport Publishing Company, 2012.

Minden, Cecilia. *Kids Can Keep Air Clean.* North Mankato, MN: Cherry Lake Publishing, 2011.

Nemeth, Jason D. *The Atmosphere.* New York, NY: PowerKids Press, 2012.

Rattini, Kristin Baird. *National Geographic Readers: Weather.* Washington, DC: National Geographic Children's Books, 2013.

## Websites

Because of the changing nature of Internet links, Rosen Publishing has developed an online list of websites related to the subject of this book. This site is updated regularly. Please use this link to access the list:

http://www.rosenlinks.com/LFO/Atmo

# INDEX